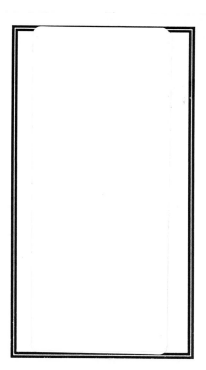

THE

EAST KENT

LIGHT RAILWAY

Vic Mitchell and Keith Smith

MP Middleton Press

*Cover picture details are
given in caption no. 112.*

*First Published June 1989
Reprinted March 1994
Second reprint June 1999*

ISBN 0 906520 61 4

© Middleton Press, 1989

Design - Deborah Goodridge

*Published by
        Middleton Press
        Easebourne Lane
        Midhurst, West Sussex
        GU29 9AZ
Tel: 01730 813169
Fax: 01730 812601*

*Printed & bound by Biddles Ltd,
        Guildford and Kings Lynn*

CONTENTS

An Ordnance Survey map of the entire route
appears opposite picture 109.

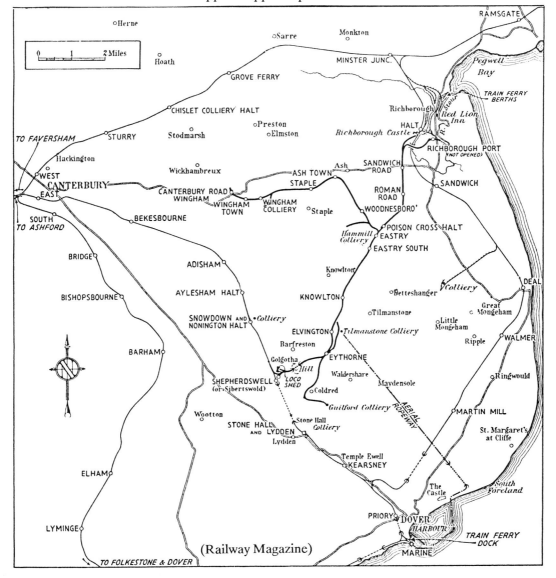

(Railway Magazine)

HISTORICAL BACKGROUND

This album is intended to illustrate the railway as built and these notes will not therefore dwell upon the numerous projected lines which are dealt with at length in most publications on the East Kent Light Railways. The plural was used in the company's title and around forty different Light Railway Orders were applied for. All the schemes related to the potential requirements of the slowly developing Kent Coalfield.

In the 1890's, borings from the 1882 Channel Tunnel shaft near Shakespeare Cliff revealed several worthwhile seams of coal and also iron. Dover Colliery was thus established (see picture 95 in our *Ashford to Dover* album) but by the end of operations in 1914, only 120 tons of coal had been raised. Borings elsewhere in East Kent encouraged investors to speculate vast sums of money and shaft sinking (usually in pairs) took many years, as worthwhile deposits were around 1500 ft. below the surface.

The East Kent Light Railways Co. Ltd. was promoted by Kent Coal Concessions Ltd. and other colliery owners in 1910. By December 1911, the first line was open for freight traffic. This was to Tilmanstone Colliery from the South Eastern & Chatham Railway's Canterbury-Dover route at Shepherdswell, which had been opened by the London Chatham and Dover Railway in 1861. By October 1912, the track had been extended to Eastry, with a branch south to Guilford Colliery. By the end of the year, the rails had reached Wingham and Hammill Collieries to the north. Shaft sinking had been retarded until the arrival of the railway, due to the devastating effect of the transport of machinery and lining bricks on the local unmetalled lanes. The advent of World War I in 1914 seriously impeded shaft sinking but Tilmanstone Colliery became productive that year.

At first only temporary lines were laid. These were sufficient to transport construction materials and to carry the early coal traffic, but it was some time before the lines reached a standard that the Board of Trade would approve for passenger traffic. Crude platforms and minimal facilities were provided, services commencing between Shepherdswell and Wingham (Colliery) on the 16th October 1916. The line was extended half a mile to Wingham Town in about 1920, although passengers were not carried officially. A massive military port was constructed by the Government in the early part of WWI at Richborough and had the EKR been able to complete its planned line to the port during the war it would have undoubtedly carried a significant part of its traffic. Unfortunately the EKR did not reach Richborough until 1928 by which time the port's fortunes had declined considerably. Plans were made to extend the railway to Canterbury and to a proposed coal export harbour to be built at Birchington, on the north coast of Kent. In the event, only a further half a mile of track was laid, ending in an incom-

GEOGRAPHICAL SETTING

Shepherdswell is situated 300 ft. above sea level, on the chalk of the eastern extension of the North Downs. After climbing through Golgotha Tunnel, the line descends onto the gentle dip slope of the chalk until reaching the gravels of the Thanet Beds in the vicinity of Eastry. The route to Wingham was largely constructed on these deposits while the branch to Richborough Port was built across the level alluvial deposits which surround the meandering River Stour, north of Sandwich.

Some clay deposits overlying the chalk are of minor economic importance for brickmaking but deep mined coal has been of major benefit, although only one pit (Betteshanger) remained functional in 1989.

ACKNOWLEDGEMENTS

In addition to the many photographers mentioned in the captions, we have received considerable help from K. Beeston (British Coal), R. Casserley, S. Garrett, I. Gotheridge, P. Hay, J. Miller, R. Randell, P. Shaw, G. T. V. Stacey, E. Staff, N. Stanyon and A. Wellard (British Coal). We are also grateful for the continued invaluable assistance given by our wives. The tickets have been kindly supplied by G. Croughton and N. Langridge.

plete cutting, north of the Canterbury Road at Wingham.

Desperate to increase income, the EKR extended passenger services along this new line and to Sandwich Road, on the Richborough branch, in November 1925. Passenger trains were banned from reaching the new station at the port due to the unsatisfactory nature of the bridges over the Southern Railway and the River Stour. The occasional passenger trains between Eastry and Sandwich Road were little used and were withdrawn on 31st October 1928. By this time the port was controlled by Pearson & Dorman Long, colliery owners, who wanted no involvement with the rickety EKR. Consequently the branch became little used.

Development of the Kent Coalfield recommenced slowly after the war and by 1926 there was sufficient optimism for the Southern Railway to feel justified in investing substantially in the EKR. Travelling habits were changing and by 1929 most miners had found more reliable methods of reaching their workplace and so workmen's trains were withdrawn that year.

For the next decade, the company derived most of its income from the movement of Tilmanstone coal, with local freight and declining passengers producing very little return. During WWII the EKR carried some ammunition to dumps in the area. In 1945, the prospect of compensation following nationalisation en-

couraged the directors to continue to operate their uneconomic venture. To their probable relief, British Railways took control on 3rd May 1948.

To reduce losses, passenger services were withdrawn entirely on 1st November 1948, the last train carrying only five people. Line closures followed thus -
27th October 1949 - - Richborough branch
25th July 1950 - - West of Eastry
1st March 1951 - - North of Eythorne
Coal traffic from Tilmanstone continued to be carried until April 1984, the line being officially closed on 31st December 1987.

In November 1985, the East Kent Railway Society was formed to save and reopen the remaining two and a quarter miles of line. By April 1989, a purchase price of £125,000 had been agreed and fund raising was proceeding.

* * * * * * *

The records of the EKR are far from complete and some facts regarding the Kent coalfield were deliberately embellished to mislead shareholders. We have consulted many knowledgeable students of the line and have endeavoured to produce the most probable account of events.

PASSENGER SERVICES

The initial timetables showed three return trips to Wingham, one to Eythorne and one to Tilmanstone, the latter two being described as workmen's trains. No public trains were operated on Sundays during the life of the line. During part of 1917, an additional service was operated to Wingham - the maximum frequency ever.

From 1918 until 1930, Wingham received three trains a day (except 1922, when there were only two) and there were two or three short workings to Eastry or Eythorne. From

about 1925 to 1930 one of these was extended to Wingham on Saturday evenings.

The Shepherdswell - Sandwich Road service was shown as two return trips in September 1925, one on every weekday for most of 1926, two on Wednesdays and Saturdays only typically in 1927 and just one trip on Saturdays by August 1928.

From 1931 until closure in 1948 there were only two journeys, at each end of the day, both running the full length of the line.

THE LOCOMOTIVES

1. No. 1 This was built by Fox Walker & Co in 1875 for the Whitland and Cardigan Railway. It became Great Western Railway no. 1386 in 1886 and was rebuilt at Swindon ten years later. It was purchased in 1911 for the Bute Docks and resold later that year to begin construction work on the EKR. It weighed a mere 25 tons and was in regular use until the early 1930s, being scrapped eventually in 1938. (D. Cullum coll.)

2. No. 2 *Walton Park* was built by Hudswell Clarke in 1908 for the Weston, Clevedon & Portishead Railway and was named after a station on that line. It worked on the Shropshire and Montgomery Railway before being transferred to the EKR in 1913. It was sold to T. W. Ward (scrap merchants in Sheffield) in 1943 but reappeared at Purfleet in working order. Later, it was reported at Hastings Gas Works and was scrapped eventually in 1957. (H. C. Casserley)

3. No. 3 was formerly London South Western Railway no. 0394 and was built by Beyer Peacock for William Adams in 1880, to Beattie's design.   Known as the "Ilfracombe Goods" owing to its suitability for working the North Devon line, it was purchased by the EKR in 1918.   The object by the leading tender axlebox is a vacuum brake cylinder and the boxes at the front were for sand.   The boiler was condemned in 1930 and scrapping took place in 1934. (H. C. Casserley)

4. No. 4 was built by Kerr, Stuart in 1917 for the Inland Waterways Docks Dept. (No. 11) from whom it was acquired by the EKR in 1919, as a replacement for *Gabrielle*. It was bought by a colliery group and leased to the EKR initially. It was transferred to the Southern Region on nationalisation in 1948 but was scrapped the following year.   It remained green painted, unlike nos. 1 to 3 which were always black, and was regarded by the staff as the best engine on the line, being used mainly for coal traffic. (H. C. Casserley)

5. No. 5   This was built by Neilson & Co in 1885 for the LSWR where it ran as no. 488. It was sold to the Ministry of Munitions in 1917 to work at the Royal Navy Salvage Depot at Ridham, near Sittingbourne, Kent.   From here it was sent to the General Stores Depot, Belvedere, in 1919 where it was put on sale the following year.   It first appeared in the EKR locomotive register in 1923.   In 1946 it was purchased by the SR to relieve its two remaining "Radials" on the Lyme Regis branch.   It was bought for £120 but over £1600 had to be spent on its extensive rebuild at Eastleigh prior to its return to service.   It was withdrawn in 1961 and purchased for preservation on the Bluebell Railway, where it can still be seen. (H. C. Casserley)

6. No. 6 was built by Sharp, Stewart in 1891 to James Stirling's O class design for the SER. It became SECR no. 372. Purchased by EKR in 1923, it was provided with a domed boiler at Ashford in 1931, giving it the class O1 specification. In 1945 it received another boiler and was painted green.   It became no. 31372 on nationalisation but was scrapped before being renumbered. (J. J. Smith)

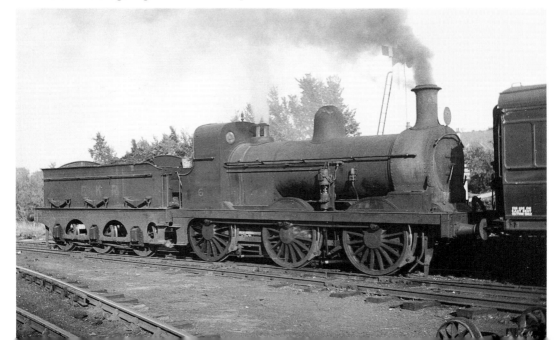

7. No. 7 was designed by Beattie and built by Beyer, Peacock in 1882 for the LSWR (No. 0127). It was commandeered by the War Office in 1917 for working a military line and was purchased by the EKR in 1926 for the bargain price of £360. It was scrapped in 1946. (Dr. I. C. Allen)

8. No. 8 Formerly SECR no. 376, this engine was of the same origin as no. 6. It arrived on the EKR in 1928 and was unsatisfactory, being broken up in 1934. (H. C. Casserley)

9. No. 100 (no. 2 from 1946) was built at Ashford in 1893 and extensively rebuilt in 1908, when it was SECR no. 383. It entered traffic on the EKR in 1935, having been overhauled and repainted at Ashford. Unfortunately the painters were not told what number to apply and so they guessed that 100 would not conflict with existing numbers. It is seen in the following year in front of sister O1, no. 6, which retained its sand boxes above the running plate and its SER style cab. In 1948, the locomotive was renumbered 31383 and remained in use until 1955. (H. C. Casserley)

10. *Gabrielle* was the only new locomotive to be ordered and the only one to be named by the company. Owing to WWI, it was probably requisitioned by the government and never delivered to the EKR. It was built by Hawthorn Leslie in 1914, to H. F. Stephen's specification. (I. Gotheridge coll)

THE ENGINEER

Holman Fred Stephens had been responsible for the design and construction of a number of light railways before being appointed engineer to the East Kent Light Railways Co. As Lt. Col. Stephens he became the line's general manager when traffic commenced and was widely known simply as "The Colonel". By 1925, the board outside his modest offices in Tonbridge included the names of the Kent & East Sussex, East Kent, West Sussex, Snailbeach, Shropshire & Montgomeryshire, Weston Clevedon & Portishead, Festiniog and Welsh Highland Railways. He died in 1931 but the East Kent continued to be administered from Tonbridge until nationalisation.

As a result of his involvement with such varied lines, there were a number of cases of locomotives being moved from one to another. Some of these are mentioned in this album and also in our *Branch Lines to Tenterden*.

The politics and finances of the group of actual and prospective collieries associated with the EKR were extremely complex and very dubious. One of the promoters had previously been bankrupt four times and it is therefore not surprising that Col. Stephens received scant remuneration for his work on the EKR after 1916. Eventually, in 1923, he was offered a large number of low value shares in the company, in lieu of payment. He became a director but had to resign from this post in 1926, to make way for SR representatives following the company's financial involvement with the railway at that time.

A selection of material from the Colonel Stephens Railway collection is displayed in the Town Museum at the top of Station Road, Tenterden. The displays include relics, tickets and photographs of many of the Colonel's lines together with his desk suitably covered with correspondence and equipment as if time had stopped still in 1931.

11. The routine office work of the EKR was carried out in the front basement room of 23 Salford Terrace, not far from Tonbridge station. For decades, there was a staff of 17 in the building, the junior having to attend to the coal fire in each office. Stephens occupied the rear office on the ground floor of the building, seen here in 1937. (R. Shepherd)

12. The frontier notice at Shepherdswell, seen in 1948. (J. H. Aston)

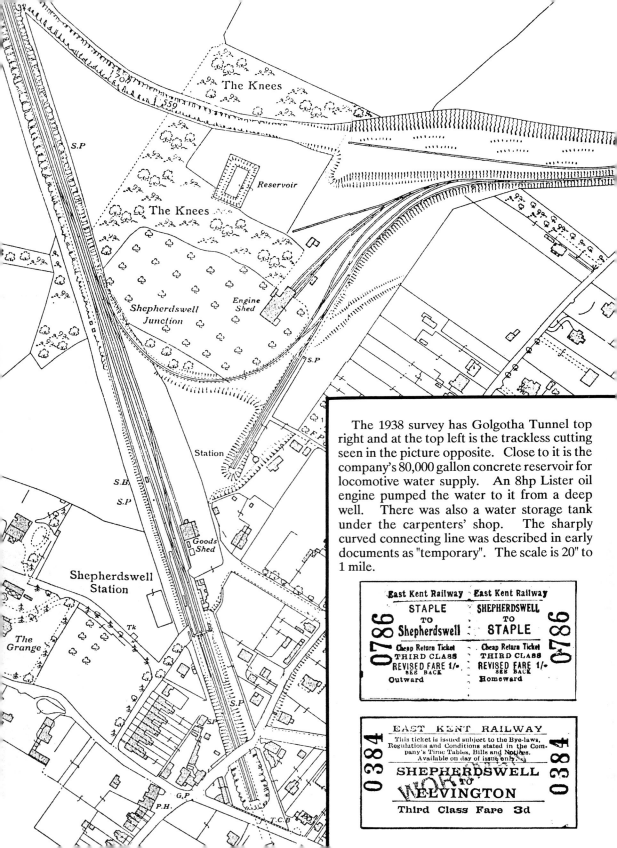

The Knees

The Knees

Reservoir

S.P

Engine Shed

Shepherdswell Junction

S.P

Station

S.B

S.P

Goods Shed

Shepherdswell Station

The Grange

Tk

S.P

S.P

G.P

P.H

T.C.B

The 1938 survey has Golgotha Tunnel top right and at the top left is the trackless cutting seen in the picture opposite. Close to it is the company's 80,000 gallon concrete reservoir for locomotive water supply. An 8hp Lister oil engine pumped the water to it from a deep well. There was also a water storage tank under the carpenters' shop. The sharply curved connecting line was described in early documents as "temporary". The scale is 20" to 1 mile.

East Kent Railway	East Kent Railway
STAPLE TO Shepherdswell	SHEPHERDSWELL TO STAPLE
Cheap Return Ticket THIRD CLASS REVISED FARE 1/- SEE BACK Outward	Cheap Return Ticket THIRD CLASS REVISED FARE 1/- SEE BACK Homeward

0786 ... 0786

EAST KENT RAILWAY
This ticket is issued subject to the Bye-laws, Regulations and Conditions stated in the Company's Time Tables, Bills and Notices. Available on day of issue only.
SHEPHERDSWELL
TO
WELVINGTON
Third Class Fare 3d

0384 ... 0384

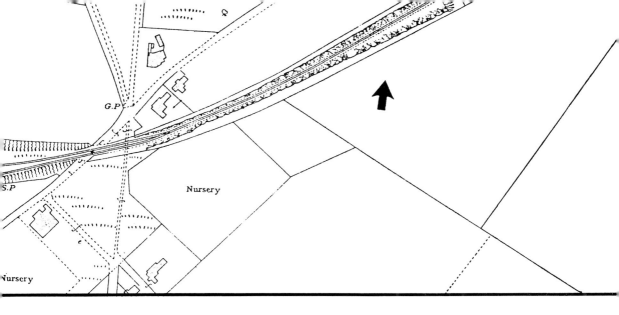

SHEPHERDSWELL - BR

13. A southward view from the end of the long down siding shows the station in the distance. The cutting on the left was made to give a direct and more level access to the EKR. When photographed in 1951, it only contained tank traps, placed there early in WWII. (D. Cullum)

14. Class O1 no. 31258 heads an REC railtour on 23rd May 1959 and runs onto the curve that links the down siding with the EKR. The van was included for the bicycles of those who wished to visit industrial railways in the area. The nearby poles were to carry overhead wires to enable electric locomotives to enter the siding without endangering shunters with a conductor rail. (R. C. Riley)

15. Later the same day, the railtour is seen departing south. The successive operators of the main line used "Shepherd's Well", while the EKR and the Ordnance Survey preferred just one word. The main building was still in use in 1989 but the goods shed had long gone. (R. C. Riley)

Freight Train Traffic - Year 1947.

Station	FORWARDED (Tons)			RECEIVED (Tons)			Receipts £
	Goods	Minerals	Coal	Goods	Minerals	Coal	
Tilmanstone	67	–	255,635	3,280	481	–	91
Eythorne	10	–	10	135	106	925	13
Woodnesborough	225	819	–	1,362	300	489	581
Eastry	127	420	94	502	371	1,687	239
Staple	1,903	1,199	–	1,374	1,547	2,121	3,390
Wingham	943	281	–	424	624	935	1,654
Totals	3,275	2,719	255,739	7,157	3,429	6,157	5,968

Livestock traffic - NIL.

Summary of Receipts - Year 1947.

	£
Passenger Traffic	26
Parcels Traffic	111
Freight Traffic	5,968
Coal from Tilmanstone Colliery } 255,635 tons @ 6d. per ton	6,391 *
Rentals from eight bungalows } and allotments	300
Total	£12,796

* Southern Railway revenue from coal in Year 1947 forwarded from Tilmanstone Colliery was £66,234, the traffic being conveyed chiefly to S.R. local stations.

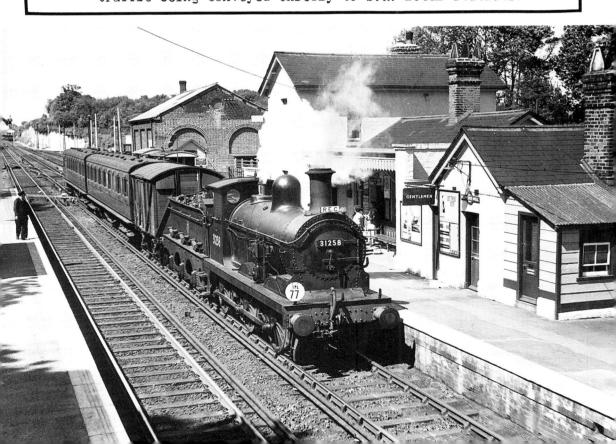

SHEPHERDSWELL - EKR

16. The high chalk embankment in the background was to form part of the direct link with the SECR but is seen in this pre-1923 photograph to be the resting place for contractor's tipping wagons. The massive chimney of no. 3 is seen outside the rustic engine shed while two telescoped wagons stand between the coaches. No. 4 is on the right while a wagon with dumb buffers stands in the platform, with the ex-LCDR Birdcage 3rd brake which was purchased in 1920.
(Col. Stephens Railway Archives)

17.   No. 3 still displayed its LSWR number when photographed with the 1.40 pm departure for Woodnesboro on 23rd January 1919. Headlamps appear in few photographs of EKR locomotives. (K. Nunn/LCGB)

18.   An October 1931 photograph features the 1905 Pickering-built ex-KESR saloon coach, no. 1, and the company's wooden office block, which appears to be ex-Army. As at Tenterden, trains arriving from the north usually stopped outside the station while the locomotive was uncoupled and run forward into a siding. The coach was then gravitated into the platform and any following wagons were run down into another siding. (H. C. Casserley)

19. The same coach was photographed from the platform on 31st December 1931, as no. 6 prepares to leave with the 12.05pm mixed train to Wingham. When the management was not present, the odd agile passenger would be invited to join the train where it was standing. (Dr. I. C. Allen)

20. No. 8 was rarely photographed, due to its short life of only six years on the line. It is seen arriving with two ex-LCDR coaches, the leading one having particularly ornate door panels. On the right is 4-4-2T no. 5. (M. D. England/NRM)

21. A mixed train has been assembled on 30th June 1934 with no. 2 *Walton Park* and ex-LCDR six-wheeler no. 10 in the lead. The iron hut to the left of the locomotive was once used for parcels and later for storing old ledgers and other documents. (H. C. Casserley)

22. Loaded coal wagons were propelled for transfer to the SR and the poor visibility on the curve resulted in a number of "incidents". The locomotive is no. 100 - another blows off outside the renovated shed.
(J. W. Sparrowe)

23. A view towards the passenger terminus on 29th July 1939 includes the connection to the SR on the right. Irregular sleeper lengths, dog spikes and light weight flat bottom rail were typical of Stephens' railways. (S. W. Baker)

24. No. 6 heads a typical mixed train on 25th April 1947, the coach being one of two ex-LSWR four compartment corridor bogie brakes, purchased in 1946. The new building on the left housed a sewage pump of no benefit to the railway, as no toilets were provided for passengers. (H. C. Casserley)

25. The buildings are larger and nearer to the SR than in photograph no. 16. They housed the booking office, the single line instrument and a public telephone. The sign on the gable refers to the latter, which was devoid of a coin box. The GPO operator recorded the cost and advised the booking clerk of the charge to be made. The 6.03pm waits to leave on Saturday 25th September 1948. (J. H. Aston)

26. The REC Railtour on 23rd May reversed into the disused platform, allowing members travelling with their bicycles to take to their wheels. Very few had witnessed the departure of the last scheduled passenger train, eleven years earlier. The platform edging and the two lines of track remained in position in 1989. (J. H. Aston)

27. A water column close to the main line was a later feature which avoided unnecessary engine movement. Nos. 31048 and 31258 were the other class O1s to normally work the branch until the end of steam. The photograph date is 8th July 1959. (J. H. Aston)

28. Another enthusiasts', railtour visited the branch on 19th November 1967 and is seen returning from Tilmanstone behind no. D6585. Coal hopper wagons are in the background and the end of the former passenger platform is on the extreme right. (S. C. Nash)

SHEPHERDSWELL SHED

29. 4-4-2T no. 5 stands by the hoist which has lost its beam. The company's workshops can be seen between the shed and the water tower.

30. Standing close to the hoist on 14th May 1927 is EKR no. 1, and in front of it is KESR no. 2 *Northiam*, which had been built by Hawthorn Leslie for the opening of that line in 1900.

The latter received its supply from a reservoir situated on high ground north of the shed. (Col. Stephens Railway Archives)

It remained on the EKR from 1921 until 1929, painted blue, and later gained fame in the film *Oh! Mr Porter*, in which it was renamed *Gladstone*. (H. C. Casserley)

31. The workshop was equipped with a 6" and a 9" lathe, a gear cutting machine, a vertical drill and overhead shafting driven by a steam engine. This was supplied from the vertical boiler in the background. The forge is on the right and in the centre is a grindstone with the treadle disconnected from its crank. Power was also supplied to a dynamo and a circular saw which was in a lean-to behind the workshop. (Col. Stephens Railway Archives)

33. Out of use on 31st December 1931 are 0-6-0ST *Walton Park*, 0-6-0 no. 8 and 0-6-0ST no. 7. In 1947 there were wagons numbered 1 to 10 and there were another six open wagons unfit for traffic. (Dr. I. C. Allen)

32. No. 8 is in steam and appears to be shunting no. 4, while ex-LCDR coaches stand on the right, along with an SR 12 ton wagon. An ash wagon is in the shed, with no. 5 nearby. The carriages on the right were out of use or awaiting repair. (F. Moore/S. C. Nash)

34. Wagon no. 41 appears to have been acquired from the LMS. Also in this 1931 photograph is the crane which originated from Ashford and was of 10-ton capacity. (H. C. Casserley)

35. When photographed in June 1934 numbers 7 and 4 stood in the open, as the southern part of the shed had disappeared by then. Assorted ferrous components protruding through brambles and nettles were typical of the various outposts of the former Stephens empire at this time. (H. C. Casserley)

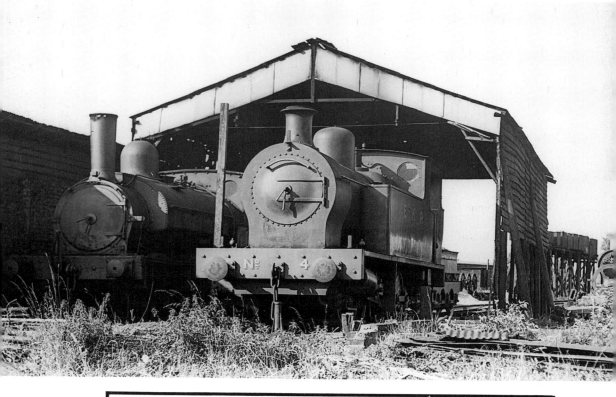

SHEPHERD'S WELL, SANDWICH ROAD, and CANTERBURY ROAD.—East Kent.

	Down.				Week Days only.								
Miles from Shepherd's Well		mrn	mrn	mrn	mrn	mrn		aft	aft	aft	aft		
348	London (Victoria)...dep.	..	8 30	..	9	5 10 34		12 10	2 10	5 15	..		
348	" (Charing Cross) "	..	..	..	..	..		..	..	..	..		
348	" (Cannon St.) "	..	..	6 16	..	..		..	..	..	..		
348	" (London B'dge) "	..	4 15	6 21	..	..		..	5 16	6 16	..		
—	Shepherd's Well......dep.	5 58	7 10	..	9 42	12 5 1 45		3 30	5 20 8 0	9 45			
1¼	Eythorne.................	6 7	7 17	..	9 48	12 12 1 52		3 37	5 27 8 9	10 2			
2½	Elvington.............. Bb	..	7 20	..	9 51	12 15 Bb		3 40	5 30 8 12	Bb			
3¼	Knowlton................	..	7 24	..	9 55	12 19		3 44	5 34 8 16	..			
5¼	Eastry, South............	..	Aa	..	Aa	Aa		Aa	Aa Aa	..			
5½	Eastry B	..	7 32	..	10 2	12 27		3 52	5 41 8 24	..			
6¼	Poison Cross Halt........	..	..	..	10 5	..		3 55	.. ..	..			
7¼	Roman Road C..........	..	..	..	10 8	..		3 58	.. ..	..			
8	Sandwich Road....... arr.	..	..	..	10 16	..		4 6	.. ..	..			
6½	Woodnesborough..........	..	7 38	..	..	12 33		..	5 45 8 28	..			
8	Ash Town................	..	7 40	..	..	12 35		..	5 50 8 34	..			
8½	Staple..................	..	7 43	..	..	12 38		..	5 54 8 39	..			
10¼	Wingham Colliery........	..	7 48	..	..	12 43		..	6 0 8 45	..			
10½	Wingham Town...........	..	7 51	..	..	12 45		..	6 3 8 48	..			
11½	Canterbury Road D.... arr.	..	7 53	..	..	12 47		..	6 5 8 50	..			

Aa Stops when required.   B Station for Sandwich.   Bb Runs to Tilmanstone Colliery Yard when required.   C Roman Road, Woodnesborough.   D Canterbury Road, Wingham.   e Except Saturdays.   L Third class only.   s Saturdays only.   X Departs at 12 30 aft. on Wednesdays.

June 1928

36. The southern end was slowly rebuilt in the mid-1930s, one new piece of timber being visible as numbers 1 and 4 wait under the new smoke hoods. In the 1920s, the carpenter spent much of his time repairing the shed but the rebuilding was undertaken by contractors. (R. C. Riley coll.)

37. From left to right, on 3rd May 1936, we see the frames of no. 2, 0-6-0 no. 6, 0-6-0T no. 4 and no. 100, apparently in running order. The end of the old shed and siding show signs of neglect. (S. W. Baker)

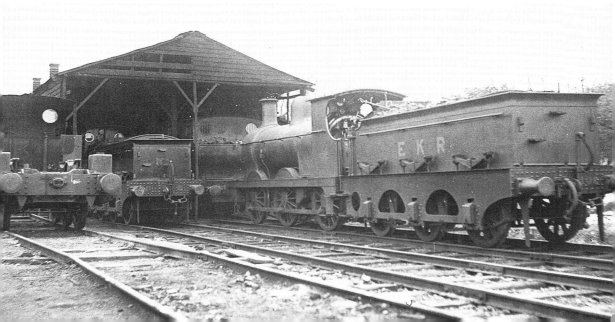

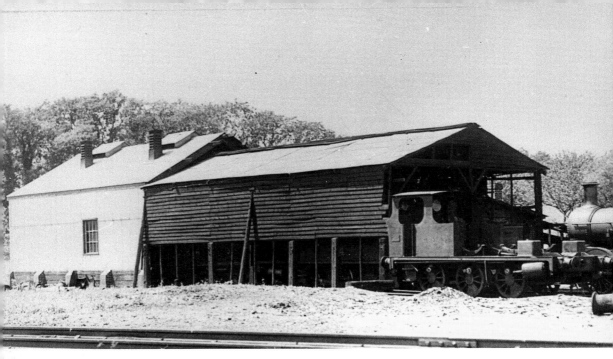

38.	By July 1936, the metamorphosis of the shed was progressing but no. 2 was still devoid of its boiler, eventually being scrapped in 1938. (H. C. Casserley)

39.   A photograph from 30th August 1938 shows the completed shed and also the Sharp Stewart 0-6-0 no. 6 undergoing repairs. Present day preservationists have not pioneered major overhauls in the open. (A. G. Wells)

40.   The scene on 4th September 1948 was much tidier as BR were quick to break up the redundant stock.   BR no. 31383 (formerly EKR no. 2 and initially 100) propels a single coach towards the platform, optimistically seeking a passenger for the evening trip.   The shed was closed soon after BR took control and thereafter class O1s ran from Dover to work the branch trains.
(S. C. Nash)

EAST OF SHEPHERDSWELL

41. The lines from the locomotive shed are in the foreground, the main line being on the extreme right. The embankment was the one built to make an easier connection with the SECR. (R. Shepherd)

42. Empties are returned to Tilmanstone by the Kerr Stuart, no. 4, and are seen from the Shepherdswell to Eythorne road in 1931. This locomotive was used almost exclusively for coal traffic, being damagingly heavy for the remainder of the line. Wagons in the high level siding are visible in the background. (Dr. I. C. Allen)

43. Having just crossed the road on 14th September 1923, no. 6 pilots the 1880 built no. 3 on the 1.17pm to Eastry. The leading wheels are on points to the high level siding. The Ilfra- combe Goods was the only tender engine to run chimney first from Shepherdswell. (K. Nunn/LCGB)

44. Looking east in 1951, we see the line to Eastry climbing beside the high level siding (extreme left), and towards the level crossing, visible in the distance. The sign states "all engines heavier than O class are prohibited from working beyond this point". (D. Cullum)

45. The railtour on 19th November 1967 was hauled to Tilmanstone by no. D6595 with no. D6585 at the other end for the return journey. The third coach is passing over North Bank crossing which appears in the previous three photographs. (S. C. Nash)

46. The chalk cutting between the level crossing and Golgotha Tunnel was subject to rockfall. The KESR 2-4-0T *Northiam* blows off as labourers pose during work on the cutting face. (R. C. Riley coll.)

47. Golgotha Tunnel is nearly half a mile long and, for most of its length, only the roof is brick lined. This is the western portal of the tunnel. The space for the second track was not fully excavated, the chalk remaining standing in massive rectangular blocks for most of the length of the tunnel. Note the poorly curved rails. (Col. Stephens Railway Archives)

48. After passing through the tunnel, the line reaches its summit and runs through this long straight cutting. The pole route for the two telegraph wires passes above the tunnel. (Col. Stephens Railway Archives)

50. In 1919, the crew of the evening train to Eastry decided to save time by not running round and propelled the single coach back to Shepherdswell. Their locomotive was no. 1, seen on the right running as an 0-4-2ST. Near Eythorne Court, they collided with no. 2 which was hauling empty wagons to Tilmanstone. The lone passenger jumped onto the grass prior to the impact - hence the open door. (I. Gotheridge coll.)

49. Looking towards Eythorne from above the eastern portal of Golgotha Tunnel on 30th May 1953, it is evident that the line had been relaid with bullhead rail. This had been carried out during WWII. The train is headed by class O1 no. 31430 and is working back from Wingham where track lifting was in progress. Any superior track materials were deposited here. (D. Cullum)

EYTHORNE

51. An early eastward view of the station's assorted huts also includes the branch to Guilford Colliery, climbing steeply in the distance. The cattle grid was necessary as no level crossing gates were provided.
(Col. Stephens Railway Archives)

52. A battered oil lamp droops on the grimy buffer beam of no. 6 as it waits with a 6-wheeled coach on 14th May 1927. Trains to and from Eastry were controlled by a Webb Thompson electric train staff. EKR locomotives were generally smart in appearance.
(H. C. Casserley)

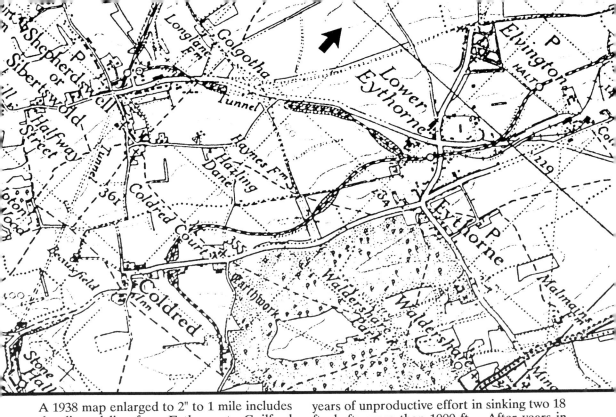

A 1938 map enlarged to 2" to 1 mile includes the disused line from Eythorne to Guilford Colliery, which is marked passing under the road north of Coldred. The colliery is not named as it was abandoned in 1921 after ten years of unproductive effort in sinking two 18 ft. shafts more than 1000 ft. After years in agricultural use, plans were made in 1989 to convert the massive engine house into eight dwellings.

53. The four-lever ground frame only worked the signals and is clearly seen in this March 1951 photograph. The track diverging to the left was relaid during WWII to accommodate a rail mounted 9.2" gun. It was on the route of the Guilford Colliery line which had been largely lifted in 1937. The earthworks for a triangular junction were started but it seems that track was not laid. (D. Cullum)

54. The loop converged at its west end at a private crossing near Eythorne Court, which for many years was the home of Mr J. E. Davenport, manager of the East Kent Colliery Co. This 1951 photograph features a tubular signal post, which added to the great variety of posts on the line. (D. Cullum)

55. Tilmanstone Colliery is in the distance but the line to it diverges to the right. It is evident that BR retained two signals in 1951, although with differing posts. The points are controlled from a ground frame beyond the crossing. (D. Cullum)

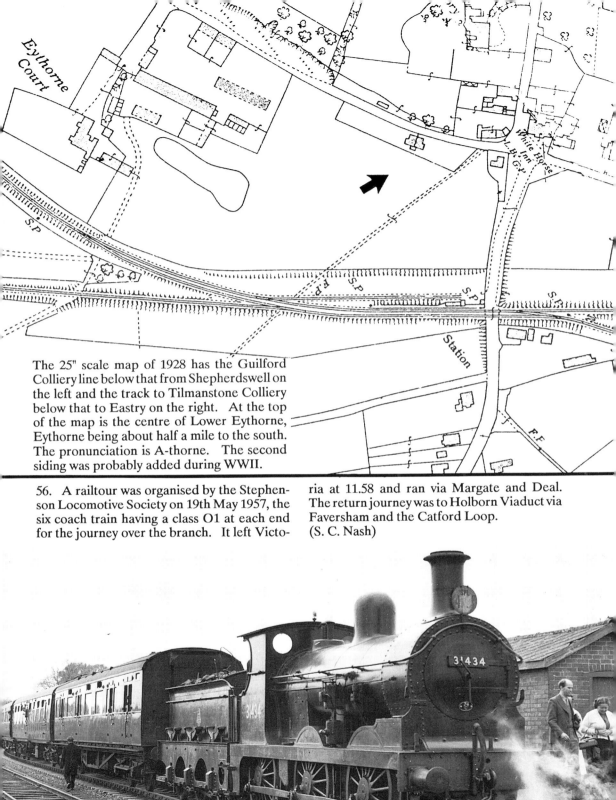

The 25" scale map of 1928 has the Guilford Colliery line below that from Shepherdswell on the left and the track to Tilmanstone Colliery below that to Eastry on the right. At the top of the map is the centre of Lower Eythorne, Eythorne being about half a mile to the south. The pronunciation is A-thorne. The second siding was probably added during WWII.

56. A railtour was organised by the Stephenson Locomotive Society on 19th May 1957, the six coach train having a class O1 at each end for the journey over the branch. It left Victoria at 11.58 and ran via Margate and Deal. The return journey was to Holborn Viaduct via Faversham and the Catford Loop.
(S. C. Nash)

57. A view of the other end of the same train shows that it included a buffet, probably the only one to have travelled over the line. The goods siding, on the left, was still in place but was soon lifted.
(S. C. Nash)

58. A glimpse from the REC Railtour on 23rd May 1959 reveals that the straight track beyond the station had been removed by then. Coal mining brought an increase in population from 1000 to 1800 between 1921 and 1931 but few used the railway. (J. H. Aston)

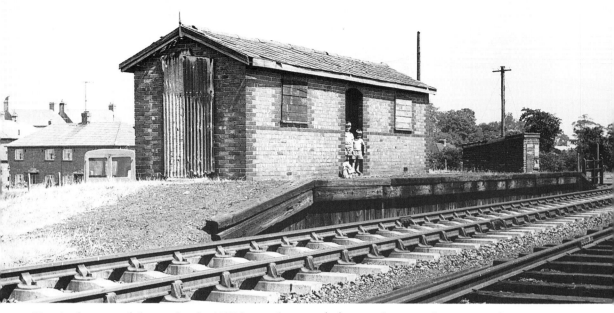

59. A close up of the station in 1959 is worth comparing with earlier views as it shows that while the platform was shortened, the accom- modation was increased. In 1948, there was a staff of one, Porter Burton, whose income was 89/6 per week, nearly £4.50. (J. H. Aston)

60. Steam traction in the Dover area ceased in 1961 and thereafter diesel shunting locomo- tives worked the coal trains. Typical is D4106, seen in May 1971 with Tilmanstone Colliery in the background. (C. Hall)

TILMANSTONE COLLIERY

61. Sinking of a 7 ft. shaft commenced in August 1906 . Three 14 ft. shafts reached a 5 ft. seam of coal at 1550 ft. down by March 1913 and this is the scene on the 12th of that month, when the mine was opened officially. H. F. Stephens is in front of the telegraph pole; the locomotive is no. 1 and the coach is ex-KESR. It was little used in the subsequent three years. (C. Harris/Col. Stephens Railway Archives)

62. No. 1 stands close to the narrow gauge colliery tracks which are surrounded by construction materials. Due to serious flooding the mine was closed for five weeks in 1914, adding to the enormous initial costs. (Lens of Sutton)

A FORECAST

KENT
COLLIERIES
LTD
250TH
ANNUAL
MEETING.

THE GENERAL MEETING OF KENT COLLIERIES, LIMITED, WAS HELD LAST TUESDAY.

The Chairman:—Gentlemen, as Director, and great grandson of one of the original shareholders, I have pleasure in calling your attention to this piece of coal, which represents nearly three centuries of patient endeavour. Owing to the fact of the world's supply of coal having become exhausted nearly a century ago, this specimen is well-nigh priceless, and will amply repay, etc,, etc , etc.

By 1920, the ability of potentially exciting holes in Kent to swallow vast amounts of capital, without return, had become a national joke.

63. Despite using the most modern techniques above and below, the colliery was almost bankrupt by December 1924. Seepage of water and the expense of pumping were a major problem. At that time 5000 tons of coal were being despatched per week and lack of wagons to move another 1000 tons was blamed on the SR.
(Col. Stephens Railway Archives)

64. The screens and washery were of the most efficient type then available but these were of no value during periods of labour unrest, such as the six month long strike in 1926. This also had a serious effect on the finances of the EKR. (Col. Stephens Railway Archives)

65. To eliminate the stranglehold that the EKR had on the colliery in respect of transport, the mine erected a £97,000 aerial ropeway to Dover where the Harbour Board built a 5000 tons capacity bunker. The five mile long ropeway passed through a tunnel near the coast and was opened on 14th February 1930. The 14.5 cwt. buckets could be loaded every 21 seconds, thus moving about 120 tons per hour. The power was from a steam engine at Maydensole but reliability of the system was low and it was little used by the mid-1930s. This is the Tilmanstone end of the ropeway in 1939. It remained standing until the 1950s. (S. W. Baker)

67. A coal briquette making plant was established at Tilmanstone, this making use of dust and material from the friable seams. Photographed on 19th June 1955 is this diesel alternative to hand shunting. (A. G. Wells)

66. On 1st January 1947, the colliery was nationalised amid much rejoicing and the music of the Betteshanger Colliery Band. The pit was labour intensive, as witnessed here by the man moving tubs on the surface. (British Coal)

68. Standard gauge shunting in May 1959 was carried out by the National Coal Board's 1955 Hunslet, works no. 4679. In 1948, up to nine trains were despatched daily, each being composed of ten wagons. (R. C. Riley)

69. Ten loaded wagons are about to depart from the colliery at 10.50 on 8th July 1959, behind class O1 no. 31425. A maximum of 40 empty wagons was permitted in the reverse direction.
(J. H. Aston)

70. Travellers on the REC Railtour on 23rd May 1959 could see both the old and new colliery headgear. Note that flat bottom rail still persisted in this area, the lines east of the road bridge belonging to the NCB.
(J. H. Aston)

71. The special train on 19th November 1967 terminated at the same location but by then the coal output had increased substantially. Diesel locomotives with bogies were an unusual sight on the line at that time. This special was probably organised by the Southern Counties Touring Society and another was run on 3rd March 1968, by the LCGB.
(S. C. Nash)

72. Substantial investment of public money in the early 1950s resulted in the concrete framed *KOEPE* winders and the new washery on the left. Photographed in 1977, the frame by the steps in the foreground was provided for a man to stand in to check the integrity of wagon floors before loading. That year the NCB received a government grant of nearly £200,000 to improve rail facilities so that almost the entire annual output of half a million tons could leave by train. The colliery closed on 24th October 1986. (British Coal)

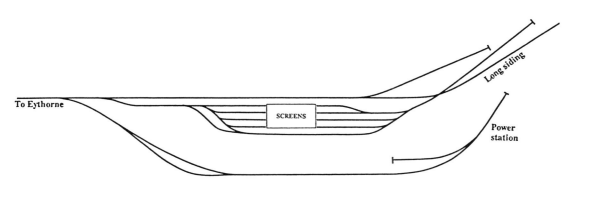

To Eythorne

Long siding

SCREENS

Power station

ELVINGTON

73. Opened as Tilmanstone Colliery Halt, it was renamed in 1925. Nearby was Elvington Court, a large country mansion which was converted to a hostel for 120 miners. Later, an estate of houses was built for the workers, who largely came from mines in other parts of Britain. Originally timber faced, part of the platform edge was still visible in 1989. (R. K. Cope/R. Carpenter)

KNOWLTON

74. Situated south of the junction of the lanes leading to Chillenden, Eastry and Betteshanger, the halt was little used. Photographed three years after the passing of the last passenger train, the structure still retained its nameboard. (D. Cullum)

EASTRY SOUTH

75. This halt was added in 1925 and was fairly conveniently situated for part of the village of about 1500 folk. The bench appears to be

76. The halt was close to the road to Hernden but to the north of Eastry South siding. This

suffering from subsidence of the platform. (R. A. Horsey/R. C. Riley coll.)

1951 panorama confirms the sparseness of the habitation. (D. Cullum)

77. Hernden is in the distance as class O1 no. 31430 returns to its demolition train at Ash, after having run to Shepherdswell for crew changing on 15th May 1954. In earlier years, rough quarried granite had arrived at the siding for inmates of the nearby workhouse (now a hospital) to make into setts for paving. (J. J. Smith)

EASTRY

78. Time was of no great importance on the EKR and timetables even less so. A complainant to the local newspaper reported that *Walton Park* seen here in 1934, was once one and a quarter hours late arriving at Wingham, having left Shepherdswell at about the correct time. (Dr. Hollick/Col. Stephens Railway Archives)

79. Three insulators on the pole indicate the extent of the telegraph system. Two wires ran to Eythorne and one to Wingham. The presence of a catch point was not complemented by any facing point locks on the passenger line. Note the six-hole fishplates with only four bolts. (C. R. L. Coles)

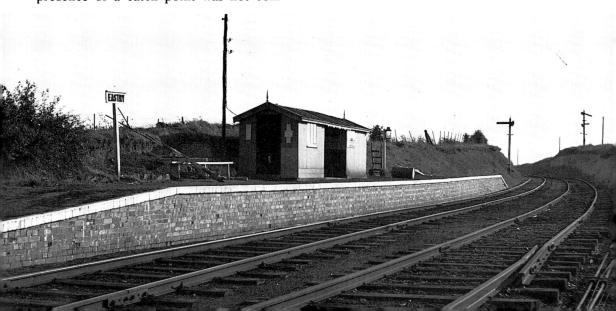

80. The EKR porter's uniform of the 1930s is on display, as is the ganger's pump trolley. Just beyond the points is the bridge over the lane to Hammill, the line to Wingham diverging to the left beyond it. The vice outside the van body suggests that it was used by permanent way staff. (C. R. L. Coles)

81. The signals at the south end of the station were still standing but out of use when photographed in 1951. By then the loop was only a siding and the up Richborough branch signal had been blown down. (D. Cullum)

82. The points at the Wingham end were removed by BR, soon after the takeover. The bridge was the only one on the main line to pass over a road and was built for double track, the handrails on the right being almost obscured by the ground frame hut. (D. Cullum)

83. A northward view in March 1951 shows the truncated loop and the line curving left to Wingham.   By then the Richborough route was returning to nature but the two embankments leading to an occupation crossing over it are visible in the fields.   The fence at the back of the left field marks the boundary of the land acquired for a triangular junction. That part of the triangle was authorised but the line on the left was never officially authorised.   Poison Cross had been close to the buildings in the distance. (J. J. Smith)

84. The 10-lever ground frame had lost its protecting hut when pictured just prior to removal, in May 1954. The interlocking mechanism is to be seen at ground level. M. L. indicated Main Line, while S. B. was for the Sandwich Branch. (J. J. Smith)

85. Track removal was progressing when recorded on 15th May 1954. The bicycle in the picture was symbolic of the future transport in the district - an era had come to an end. After closure, the nearest station for Ham was at Sandwich. (S. C. Nash) HAMMILL

1. DOWN STOP
2 DOWN STARTER
3 LOOP SIGNAL
4 POINTS LOOP TOP
5   "   "   BOTTOM.
6 POINTS. S.B. PULL 2.
7 DUMMY SIGNAL
8 UP STOP. S.B.
9 UP STARTER.
10 UP STOP M.L

RICHBOROUGH BRANCH

The 1938 survey is shown at 2" to 1 mile with the SR Ramsgate to Deal line running from top to bottom. The EKR junction at Eastry is lower left and the positions of the halts on the Richborough branch have been added.

POISON CROSS

86.   The loop commenced between two un-gated crossings.   It had a siding trailing off it which is largely hidden by grass on the extreme left of this 1951 northward view.   Nearby is the district of Gore, the bizarre name resulting from deaths at the Reformation.   (J. J. Smith)

ROMAN ROAD

87.   Another look north in 1951 shows the long defunct halt which was close to the Sandwich-Woodnesborough road.   The Roman road from Dover crossed the line at Poison Cross. (J. J. Smith)

SANDWICH ROAD

88. The smoke from no. 7 is blown down as it stands on the windswept flats surrounding the much-meandering River Stour, on 22nd September 1928. After running round its coaches, the locomotive would haul them over the level crossing and return to the platform. (Lens of Sutton)

90. Not surprisingly the EKR bridge over the SR was not approved for passenger traffic. Castle sidings were at the foot of Richborough Hill, seen on the left. Gravel and sugar beet were sometimes loaded here, as was Blue Stonar from a nearby pit. This was used in pottery manufacture. (Col. Stephens Railway Archives)

89. Looking north, across the A257 in March 1951, we see the only level crossing gates on the line and an advertisement hoarding which probably brought more revenue than the station did. Over the road is a gate to the goods yard which was the site of the loop seen in the previous picture. Freight facilities were officially withdrawn on 1st January 1950. (J. J. Smith)

The 1938 map at 25" to 1 mile includes the fan
of three sidings at Richborough Castle.   The
line on the right continues to the Port.

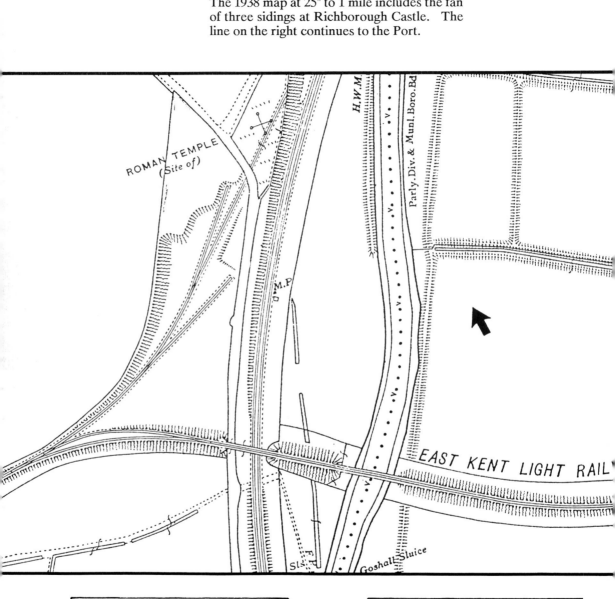

91. The bridge over the River Stour had been built in 1928 with "temporary wooden trestles" instead of an opening span as required by the Authorizing Order. A fixed bridge was agreed with the Water Authority in 1931. (R. Shepherd)

EAST KENT RAILWAY
This ticket is issued subject to the Bye-laws, Regulations and Conditions stated in the Company's Time Tables, Bills and Notices. Available on day of issue only.
EASTRY SOUTH
TO
ELVINGTON
THIRD CLASS _____ FARE 6d
Williamson, Ticket Printer, Ashton-u-Lyne
0343

The EKR from Eastry is lower left and the sidings from the SR are at the top of the 1938 survey, reproduced at 20" to 1 mile. The terminal platform was below the words *Richborough Port*.

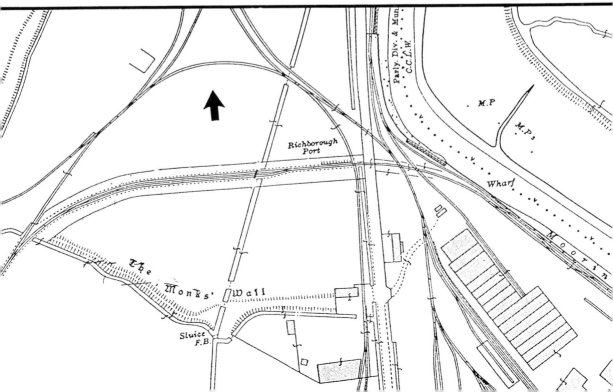

92. The station was completed in anticipation of passenger services commencing but no fares were collected here. The A256 coast road passes over the line beyond the cattle grid - hence the advertisement boards.
(Lens of Sutton)

93. Unclear in the previous photograph is the level crossing of one of the dock lines. During WWI, the buildings in the distance had been used for making blocks for the extension of Dover Harbour.
(Col. Stephens Railway Archives)

→

95. S. Pearson, Lord Cowdray's construction company, carried out improvements to Dover Harbour in the early part of the century and in 1925 combined with Dorman Long, owners of Betteshanger Colliery, to develop Richborough as a coal export port. The EKR's dream of carrying large quantities of coal to the ships never came true, although some Snowdown coal was carried around 1929. It is reputed that some sugar beet was taken to the waterside and that batches of Norwegian pit props were carried fairly regularly. P & DL's *St. Anselm* is seen in store on 7th October 1953.
(A. G. Wells)

94.   The importance of Richborough Port in WWI cannot be overemphasized and it will be considered more fully in a future album. There were very extensive army and civilian camps near the port, as well as ship building yards.   At the north end of the site, a train ferry terminal came into use on 10th February 1918 and this is seen from the bridge of TF1, the unimaginative "name" given to the first train ferry.   (I. Gotheridge coll.)

RICHBOROUGH ESTATE
DANGER·KEEP OUT
You Have Been
WARNED

WOODNESBORO

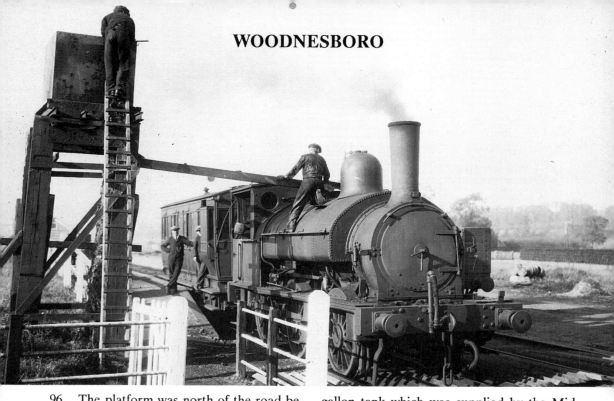

96.   The platform was north of the road between Snowdown and Woodnesborough, the centre of which was three quarters of a mile to the east.   No. 7 is taking water from the 500 gallon tank which was supplied by the Mid Kent Water Co.   Col. Stephens preferred to use "free water", pumped by the railway. (D. S. Barrie/S. C. Nash coll.)

97.   The population of the village was under 900 and so the platform length was more than generous. The station was unstaffed in the last years of operation.   (Lens of Sutton)

98. The single siding connected south of the road, seen here in 1939. Further south, a half mile long line branched off to Hammill Brick Works. This was established in the buildings of an abortive colliery, the shafts of which were never started. At the junction of this line, a buffer food store was erected at the end of WWII. This also generated rail traffic for some years after the war. (S. W. Baker)

EAST KENT RAILWAY
This ticket is issued subject to the Bye-laws, Regulations and Conditions stated in the Company's Time Tables, Bills and Notices Available on day of issue only.
STAPLE
TO
WOODNESBORO'
Third Class Fare 4½d

The Hammill Brick Company was established in 1926 on the site of the proposed Hammill Colliery. The works was very modern for its period and was established to produce hard ceramic paving blocks for the road building market.

The market for the product did not materialise and the works was rapidly changed over to the production of facing bricks. The Company has continued the production of high quality facing bricks throughout its history. A new plant has recently been installed for the production of traditional stock bricks which will enable the Company to supply bricks very similar to the old handmade Kent red stocks.

ASH TOWN

East Kent Rly.
Cheap Day Ticket
WOODNESBORO'
TO
Staple
3rd Return Fare 4½d.
Homeward Journey
See Back
0194

East Kent Railway
ASH
TO
SHEPHERDSWELL
RETURN TICKET
THIRD CLASS
RETURN FARE 1/8
SEE BACK
Outward
0199

99. Access was by footpath from the village which can be seen in the distance. With over 2000 inhabitants, it would have been a potential source of revenue until the advent of buses. (D. Cullum)

100. On 8th May 1954, track lifting had nearly reached Poulton Farm siding, which was south of the line, west of Ash. East of Ash another agricultural siding had been provided, for Moat Farm, on the north side. No. 31434 was working the train. (J. J. Smith)

STAPLE

101. This is the view from a Wingham bound mixed train on 9th September 1936. A wind pump was the preferred but unreliable method of obtaining a free water supply for locomotives. (S. W. Baker)

102. Staple handled twice as much freight as Wingham and at least ten times more than each of the other stations, flowers, fruit and vegetables being the main goods outward. (R. Shepherd)

EAST KENT RAILWAY.

This Ticket is issued subject to the Bye-Laws Regulations and Conditions stated in the Company's Time Tables, Bills and Notices.

Available on day of issue only.

ASH TOWN
TO
STAPLE

Third Class   Fare-3½d.

379

379

103. During WWII, a vast ammunition store was established on the nearby RAF station. To increase office space in connection with this special traffic, coach no. 3 was grounded by the platform. It was ex-Cheshire Lines Committee. Enemy agents were not likely to suspect its real use - the sandbagged air-raid shelter was a common sight then. (Lens of Sutton)

104. The driver of no. 6 pauses amongst the empty vegetable boxes, on his way to Wingham with a mixed train on 25th April 1947. There were few passengers, as the village of under 500 people was three quarters of a mile to the south. (H. C. Casserley)

105. An eastward view in October 1950 shows the weighted point levers and the rural location of the station. In the last year of the EKR, Porter Epps was the solitary member of staff here. (D. Cullum)

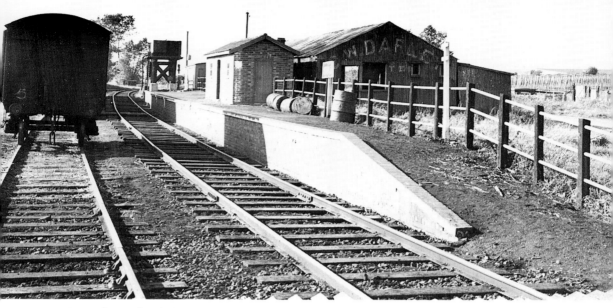

106. The station building and platform being constructed in brick gave an impression of relative importance. The corrugated iron structure was used by C. W. Darley Ltd, wholesale vegetable merchants. (D. Cullum)

107. In 1947, no passenger tickets were issued but 997 parcels were despatched and 220 were received, in addition to a considerable wagon load traffic. The windpump had disappeared and traffic had ceased nine months before this photograph was taken in March 1951. (J. J. Smith)

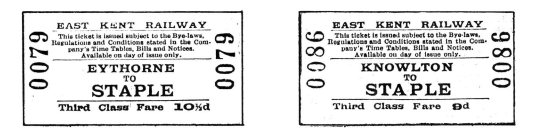

EAST KENT RAILWAY
This ticket is issued subject to the Bye-laws, Regulations and Conditions stated in the Company's Time Tables, Bills and Notices. Available on day of issue only.
EYTHORNE
TO
STAPLE
Third Class Fare **10½d**
0079

EAST KENT RAILWAY
This ticket is issued subject to the Bye-laws, Regulations and Conditions stated in the Company's Time Tables, Bills and Notices. Available on day of issue only.
KNOWLTON
TO
STAPLE
Third Class Fare **9d**
0986

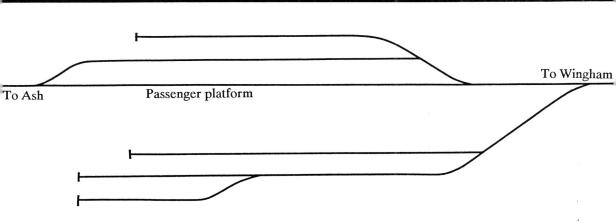

To Ash

Passenger platform

To Wingham

108. The pump trolley, with handle broken, stood at the end of the sidings in 1953, a monument to much labour in vain. (A. G. Wells)

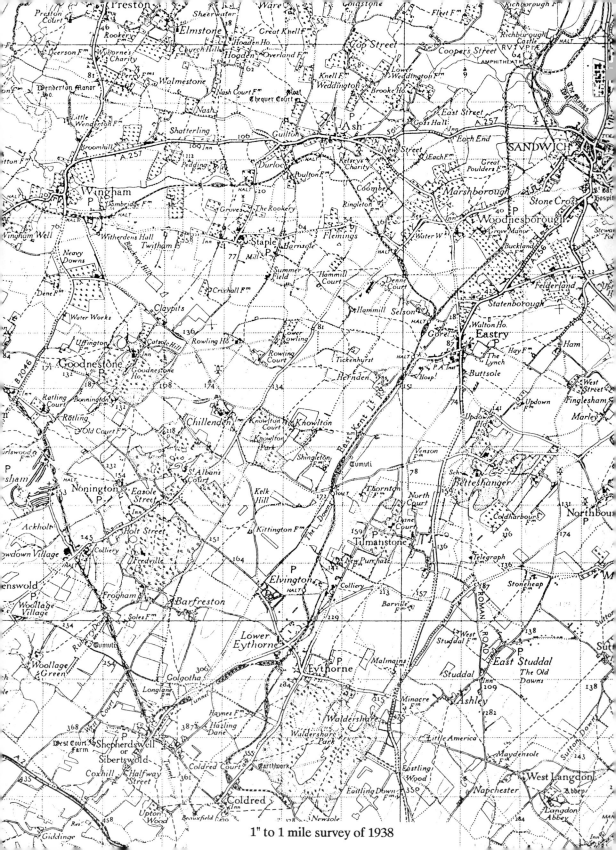

1" to 1 mile survey of 1938

WINGHAM COLLIERY

109.   The platform, on the north side of the line and east of the Wingham - Staple road, was opened in 1916 and photographed in October 1950.   Initially, a siding southwards towards the colliery was provided but shaft sinking did not proceed beyond 50ft., due to WWI.   This siding was east of the halt.   The substantial pit head buildings were erected in brick and are now used by an animal feedstuff factory and shop.   The line was extended to Wingham Town during 1920 and until then trains had to run back half a mile to reach a run-round loop. Note the unusual use of bullhead rail.
(D. Cullum)

110.   400yds. west of the halt, the Wingham Engineering Company's siding diverged to the south and is seen here in 1953.   General engineers, the firm was much involved with agricultural steam engines, substantial quantities of steel arriving by rail. (J. J. Smith)

WINGHAM TOWN

111.   The terminus was provided with a loop which appears to have been photographed soon after it came into use in about 1920.   It appears that passengers were carried without official approval for around five years.   No. 2 may lack lustre but it was thirdhand.   The Sessions House is in the background, Wingham being a small but important town of great antiquity.   (Lens of Sutton)

112. A period action shot of the driver peering over his walrus moustache as the young lady inserts her infant into its perambulator, while the guard/shunter jumps down to uncouple no. 3, the former "Ilfracombe Goods".
(Lens of Sutton)

The 1937 survey at 15" to 1 mile includes all three Wingham stations, although marked as halts.

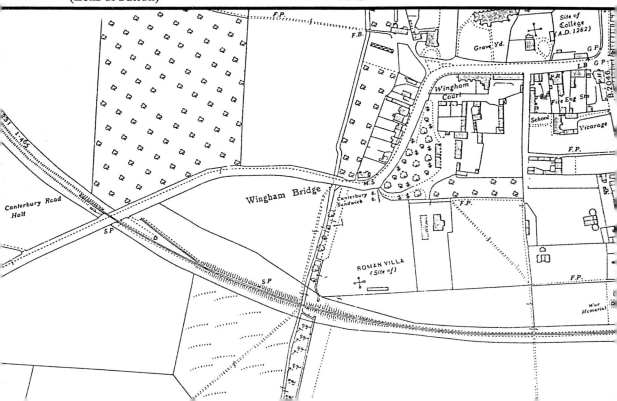

113.   The station was down graded in 1925
when the line was extended 770yds. to Canterbury Road.   The loop and siding were
removed and the bathing hut type building,
seen in the previous two photographs, was
moved to the new terminus.   (Lens of Sutton)

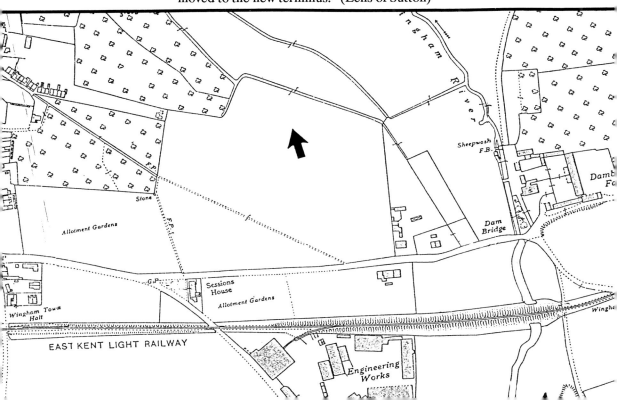

WINGHAM CANTERBURY ROAD

114. Looking towards Wingham Town, we see the final curve on the railway where it passed the huts of a WWII army camp. This embankment and one west of the Wingham Colliery remain as the only evidence of the EKR near Wingham. (H. C. Casserley)

116. As at Shepherdswell, the coaches usually arrived in the platform under gravity while the locomotive waited in the siding. No. 7 is ready to depart but was quite likely to shunt the coaches into the siding to attach some wagons behind them. (Lens of Sutton)

The December 1938 timetable was typical of the period 1930-48.

SHEPHERD'S WELL, SANDWICH ROAD, and CANTERBURY ROAD—East Kent—(Week Days only.)

Miles	Down	mrn		aft	aft			Miles from Sandwich Rd	Up	mrn		aft	aft		NOTES
	348 London (Victoria)...dep.	..	..	2 10	3 20	..			Canterbury Road D...dep.	8 40		6 10	6 32	..	
	348 " (Charing C) "	...	...	...	...	...		1	Wingham Town............	8 42		6 12	6 34		
	348 " (Cannon St) "	...	...	...	...	...		1	Wingham Colliery.........	8 45		6 15	6 37		NOTES
	348 " (Lndn Bdge) "	3413		...	...	...		2¼	Staple....................	8 52		6 22	6 44		
	Shepherd's Well.......dep.	7 30		4 45	5 45	..		3¼	Ash Town.................	8 55		6 26	6 47		A Station for Beckley and Sandhurst
1¼	Eythorne.................	7 37		4 52	5 51	..		4¼	Woodnesborough..........	8 59		6 30	6 51		A Arr. 9.55 mrn.
2¼	Elvington................	7 40		4 55	5 54			—	Sandwich Rd........dep.	...		...	...		Aa Stops when required
3¼	Knowlton.................	7 43		4 59	5 58			—	Roman Road C..........	...		...	...		B Station for Sandwich
6¼	Eastry, South............	..		Aa	Aa	..		—	Poison Cross Halt........	...		...	...		B Arr. Hastings 7 19 on Sats.
5¼	Eastry B.................	7 51		5 7	6 43			5¼	Eastry B.................	9 5		6 35	6 55		C Roman Rd, Woodnesborough
6¼	Poison Cross Halt........	..		..	..	..		6	Eastry, South............	..		Aa	Aa	..	D Canterbury Rd, Wingham
7¼	Roman Road C...........	..		..	..	..		7¼	Knowlton.................	9 15		Aa	Aa	..	E or E Except Sats
8	Sandwich Road.......arr.	..		..	..	..		8¼	Elvington................	9 19		6 48	7 7		F Arr 8 mins earlier on Sats
6¼	Woodnesborough.........	7 55		5 11	6 8	..		9¼	Eythorne.................	9 23		6 52	7 11		H 3rd class only
8	Ash Town................	7 58		5 15	6 12	..		11¼	8 Shepherd'sW'll 348,359 arr.	9 30		6 59	7 18		J Arr. 10 mins. earlier.
8¼	Staple...................	8 2		5 18	6 16	..		80	76¾ 359 London (Lndn Bdge) arr.	1146 Y		11 4	11 4		S or S Sats only
10¼	Wingham Colliery........	8 8		5 23	6 21			80¾	77¼ 359 " (Cannon St) "	1155 F		...	...		Y Arr 5 mins earlier on Sats.
10¼	Wingham Town...........	8 10		5 25	6 24			81¼	78¼ 359 " (Charing C) "	...		1110	1110		
11¼	Canterbury Road D.... arr.	8 12		5 27	6 26			83	79¼ 359 " (Victoria)... "	1127		1024 J	1021		

115. Looking in the other direction, the terminus comes into sight. Plans for an extension to Canterbury did not come to fruition, although some of the land was acquired and fenced. (D. Cullum)

117.   The pointed building between the wagons was an ex-WWI army hut which served as a goods shed, a similar one standing at Shepherdswell.   It was circular, made of iron, and lasted until 1946 when it was replaced by a van body.   The coach was often not brought into the platform, passengers being invited to leap to the ground or climb up, using a sack barrow as a ladder.
(R. Cope/Col. Stephens Railway Archives).

118. The hut sections from Wingham Town were reassembled in a different order. Later the nameboard was larger and more honest, admitting that it was Canterbury Road. During WWII the line was extended by about 150yds. but the reason has not been recorded. (Lens of Sutton)

119. The windswept and deserted station, illustrated in 1939, was at least on a main road (A257) and thus convenient for the transport of goods to and from the railhead. Mr. Dick Harffey was the last employee and was designated "station agent", a term used elsewhere in the Stephens empire. (S. W. Baker)

120. By 1953 only the signals, their levers, the telegraph pole and the honest nameboard remained. Thus ended one of the most curious chapters in railway history. Had coal mining been more successful, the line could have been Col. Stephens most profitable, instead of becoming one of his greatest disappointments. (J. J. Smith)

Middleton Press

Easebourne Lane, Midhurst, W Sussex. GU29 9AZ Tel: 01730 813169 Fax: 01730 812601
If books are not available from your local transport stockist, order direct with cheque,
Visa or Mastercard, post free UK.

BRANCH LINES
Branch Line to Allhallows
Branch Lines around Ascot
Branch Line to Ashburton
Branch Lines around Bodmin
Branch Line to Bude
Branch Lines around Canterbury
Branch Lines around Chard & Yeovil
Branch Line to Cheddar
Branch Lines around Cromer
Branch Lines to Effingham Junction
Branch Lines around Exmouth
Branch Line to Fairford
Branch Line to Hawkhurst
Branch Line to Hayling
Branch Lines to Horsham
Branch Line to Ilfracombe
Branch Line to Kingswear
Branch Lines to Launceston & Princetown
Branch Lines to Longmoor
Branch Line to Looe
Branch Line to Lyme Regis
Branch Lines around March
Branch Lines around Midhurst
Branch Line to Minehead
Branch Line to Moretonhampstead
Branch Lines to Newport (IOW)
Branch Line to Padstow
Branch Lines around Plymouth
Branch Line to Selsey
Branch Lines around Sheerness
Branch Line to Swanage *updated*
Branch Line to Tenterden
Branch Lines to Torrington
Branch Lines to Tunbridge Wells
Branch Line to Upwell
Branch Lines around Weymouth
Branch Lines around Wimborne
Branch Lines around Wisbech

NARROW GAUGE BRANCH LINES
Branch Line to Lynton
Branch Lines around Portmadoc 1923-46
Branch Lines around Porthmadog 1954-94
Two-Foot Gauge Survivors
Romneyrail

SOUTH COAST RAILWAYS
Ashford to Dover
Bournemouth to Weymouth
Brighton to Eastbourne
Chichester to Portsmouth
Dover to Ramsgate
Eastbourne to Hastings
Hastings to Ashford
Portsmouth to Southampton
Southampton to Bournemouth
Worthing to Chichester

SOUTHERN MAIN LINES
Bromley South to Rochester
Charing Cross to Orpington
Crawley to Littlehampton
Dartford to Sittingbourne
East Croydon to Three Bridges
Epsom to Horsham
Exeter to Barnstaple
Exeter to Tavistock
Faversham to Dover

London Bridge to East Croydon
Orpington to Tonbridge
Tonbridge to Hastings
Salisbury to Yeovil
Swanley to Ashford
Tavistock to Plymouth
Victoria to East Croydon
Waterloo to Windsor
Waterloo to Woking
Woking to Portsmouth
Woking to Southampton
Yeovil to Exeter

EASTERN MAIN LINES
Fenchurch Street to Barking

COUNTRY RAILWAY ROUTES
Andover to Southampton
Bath to Evercreech Junction
Bournemouth to Evercreech Jn.
Burnham to Evercreech Junction
Croydon to East Grinstead
Didcot to Winchester
East Kent Light Railway
Fareham to Salisbury
Frome to Bristol
Guildford to Redhill
Porthmadog to Blaenau
Reading to Basingstoke
Reading to Guildford
Redhill to Ashford
Salisbury to Westbury
Stratford Upon Avon to Cheltenham
Strood to Paddock Wood
Taunton to Barnstaple
Wenford Bridge to Fowey
Westbury to Bath
Woking to Alton
Yeovil to Dorchester

GREAT RAILWAY ERAS
Ashford from Steam to Eurostar
Clapham Junction 50 years of change
Festiniog in the Fifties
Festiniog in the Sixties
Isle of Wight Lines 50 years of change
Railways to Victory 1944-46
SECR Centenary album

LONDON SUBURBAN RAILWAYS
Caterham and Tattenham Corner
Charing Cross to Dartford
Clapham Jn. to Beckenham Jn.
East London Line
Finsbury Park to Alexandra Palace
Holborn Viaduct to Lewisham
Kingston and Hounslow Loops
Lewisham to Dartford
Lines around Wimbledon
London Bridge to Addiscombe
North London Line
South London Line
West Croydon to Epsom
West London Line
Willesden Junction to Richmond
Wimbledon to Epsom

STEAMING THROUGH
Steaming through Cornwall
Steaming through Kent

Steaming through West Hants
Steaming through West Sussex

TRAMWAY CLASSICS
Aldgate & Stepney Tramways
Barnet & Finchley Tramways
Bath Tramways
Bournemouth & Poole Tramways
Brighton's Tramways
Camberwell & W.Norwood Tramways
Clapham & Streatham Tramways
Dover's Tramways
East Ham & West Ham Tramways
Edgware and Willesden Tramways
Eltham & Woolwich Tramways
Embankment & Waterloo Tramways
Enfield & Wood Green Tramways
Exeter & Taunton Tramways
Gosport & Horndean Tramways
Greenwich & Dartford Tramways
Hammersmith & Hounslow Tramways
Hampstead & Highgate Tramways
Hastings Tramways
Holborn & Finsbury Tramways
Ilford & Barking Tramways
Kingston & Wimbledon Tramways
Lewisham & Catford Tramways
Liverpool Tramways 1. Eastern Routes
Liverpool Tramways 2. Southern Routes
Maidstone & Chatham Tramways
North Kent Tramways
Portsmouth's Tramways
Reading Tramways
Seaton & Eastbourne Tramways
Shepherds Bush & Uxbridge Tramways
Southampton Tramways
Southend-on-sea Tramways
Southwark & Deptford Tramways
Stamford Hill Tramways
Thanet's Tramways
Victoria & Lambeth Tramways
Waltham Cross & Edmonton Tramways
Walthamstow & Leyton Tramways
Wandsworth & Battersea Tramways

TROLLEYBUS CLASSICS
Croydon Trolleybuses
Bournemouth Trolleybuses
Hastings Trolleybuses
Maidstone Trolleybuses
Reading Trolleybuses
Woolwich & Dartford Trolleybuses

WATERWAY ALBUMS
Kent and East Sussex Waterways
London to Portsmouth Waterway
Surrey Waterways
West Sussex Waterways

MILITARY BOOKS and VIDEO
Battle over Portsmouth
Battle over Sussex 1940
Blitz over Sussex 1941-42
Bombers over Sussex 1943-45
Bognor at War
Military Defence of West Sussex
Secret Sussex Resistance
Sussex Home Guard
War on the Line
War on the Line VIDEO

OTHER BOOKS
Betwixt Petersfield & Midhurst
Changing Midhurst
East Grinstead Then & Now
Garraway Father & Son
Index to all Stations
South Eastern & Chatham Railways
London Chatham & Dover Railway